DEEP PRESS ON

DEEP PRESS ON

POEMS

KEITH EDWARD SOWELL

ACKNOWLEDGEMENTS

This collection of poetry is written in 2 sections to highlight the focus on the fall into depression, and distinguish the navigation and grappling with it alongside anxiety and faith. The first, "DEEP," conveys the descent through themes of isolation, suicidal thoughts, and identifying the mental health issue. The second, "PRESS ON," depicts adapting to the ongoing battle with motivation, belief and vulnerability. My hope is that this book helps those that come across it in some form. Whether it be: encouraging the weary soul to push a little further, empowering those going through in silence to share their load, motivating readers to check on those around them, and/or helping anyone along their faith walk.

All praise to God, from whom I received the message of this book.

I have endless gratitude towards Brandon Leake, Fariss Ryan and Eva Milan for all they have taught and assisted me with in bringing this creation to reality.

I am forever thankful to my parents, siblings, grandmother, nieces, nephews, aunts, uncles, and all of my family for their continuous support. To Senior Pastor Margaret Kelly, Reverend Dr. James Kelly, and my Changing Your Life Ministries family for raising the foundation of my faith. I am beyond honored for all that the Gray's Creek schools and Duke University have instilled in me. Forever grateful for all the friends from each of these institutions, and other areas of life who have helped mold who I am.

I have immense appreciation for Mr. Joel Mayo, Ms. Nicole Rivers, and the Gray's Creek Poetic Pathos team for starting me on my poetic journey. As well as Ms. Kimberly McCrae, and my slam teammates Adriana Parker, Michael Ivory, and Ashley Benn who have all cultivated my craft as coaches at Duke.

Lastly, I am thankful for Duke Spoken Verb, all that have allowed me to write and grow alongside them, and those that have directly impacted my writing as a poet, including: Gaelyn Dent, Dara Sontan, Allayne Thomas, Marie-Line Lochard, Chris Poon, Dorothy Adu-Amankwah, Pranav Athimuthu, Kyra Citron, Nefer Batsuli Rezilience Williamson, Maram Elnagheeb, and Jamal Burns.

TABLE OF CONTENTS

DEEP

DEEP

Elevated
When you are so high up
The deepest valleys are
Nonexistent

Summit
Where the only thing you feel
More than the cold is
Descent

Heavy
Burdens return from their break
Weight has found its
Presence

Sink
Clogged but leaking
Drowning even with water's
Absence

Low
Farther in the hole
The only way to go is
Down

So
Below the sea level
Gravity has given
Up

Ask
Why is depth
1 letter off from
Death

Abyss
Will it take being 6 feet
To escape being this
Deep

HEAVY

I don't remember
When it started
But the difference
Is hard to forget

Getting up from bed
Sleepy
Later getting up
Sluggish

Something on my
Shoulders
Nothing on my
Skin

Waking up
Each day
Heavier
Than the last

8:30's became maybes
Fridays looked like Mondays
March turned to April
And it was still there

With me in class
With me in church
Slept to make it better
That made it worse

This was a weight
That you couldn't weigh
I continued to wait
For it to be lifted

But it wouldn't

Only thing more heavy
Than carrying it
Is calling it out
By name

PRESSURE

The deeper you dive
The greater the pressure

There's a point in the ocean
Where lungs collapse
In theory

100 atm is the human limit
Yet in front of an ATM
At this moment it is hard

To withdraw breath with
Nothing deposited
An unhealthy exchange

Be it unsustainable wealth
Physical or mental health
Panic rushes in

Blocking forward movement
An attack like the Red Sea
When bloody rivers flow

We are taught to apply pressure
We cover the site of the wound
For healing to begin

What if pressure causes the injury?

A smothered fire
Burns out into
The dead of night

A lifted soul
With a lightened load
Will see the light of day

As I ponder
Letting go of what kept me grounded
I wonder

How hard is breathing
till the releasing
of a diamond?

ASHES

You said follow the light
You are the light
I can see

Then I saw the fire
Reached out for the fire
To make ends meet

I made a torch of the branch
That You gave to me
Let the flames get too close
To this olive tree

They burned my seeds
Now it's ash I reap

You said look towards the sky
My limits were the sky
I can soar

Then I saw the sun
Tried to fly with the sun
To burn as bright

I made a torch of the canvas
That You gave to me
Let the flames get too close
To the painting I made

They burned my seams
Now it's ash I reap

DECREASE

Decrease
To be failing in energy
Is to run on empty
Body yielding
Falling

Decrease
In sanity and mental stability
Normal be distant memory
Always on
Edge

Decrease
Finances so liquid they flow
Tossed to and fro between
Overflow and an
Overdraft

Decrease
Getting less sleep each passing day
Escaping the nightmare
Waking up in
Another

Decrease
For it is never known
How many years
These tears
Cost

Until it is too late

SILENCE

When I hear the silence …

I retreat to the deepest crevice of my mind.
Seeking out solace in solitude.

I'm an introvert,
which surprises some people.

But I talk so much at times
because I'm afraid of the silent pauses in conversations.

It is through them, that I can fade so far into the background
that I must ask myself if I exist.

I talk so loud to fill the emptiness.
Finding refuge in volume.

My voice gets lost in silence.
I forget what it sounds like.

But it's in that same silence,
where I hear my heart beating again.

Which means I'm technically alive.

Life can get a little lively.
Can get a little loud.

One minute I'm begging for silence.
Next minute I'm scared,

because that's where my depression thrives.
Where it revives without me knowing.

Weird, that quietness brings headaches into my life.
How nothingness fills all roles.

I think, sleep, cry
in quiet.

I shout, pray, worship
in private.

I lose myself, yet
I am rediscovered in calmness.

I'm broken, yet
Made whole in stillness.

It is in silence
Where I find my God …

… or find a dead end.
Just depends on the day.

CHAMELEON

I've never seen a chameleon
Yet I've felt its burden

The impulse to sit still
When caught by the lens of fear
The film becomes too real
So fade to black

Camouflage
Is thought to keep safe
But no one comes to save
When the pain blends in

I've learned to bandage
All of the damage
But no amount of coverage
Heals internal bleeding

Cleaning these wounds
Would risk infection
And there's no such thing
As a brain transplant

I replace the pain
With something more vain
Denial is the best
Anesthesia

I have known
From firsthand
Experience
This doesn't work

For I too have felt
What it's like to be ignored
Pushed to the background
As a protagonist's prop

Yet here I stand front and center

I don't expect
The pain to heal
Beneath the gauze
But it's easier to look at

The chameleon and I
Are alike in this way
Between falling prey
Or being cast away

We choose the latter
To keep as many
Pieces of ourselves
From being consumed

It is possible
For both to happen
Nevertheless
Until that happens

I try to remember
Though not visible
At least this vessel
Is still alive

CONVERGENCE

A rock
A hard place
Stuck in
The in-between

From the moment we draw breath
We teeter on a seesaw
Opposing sides of life and death
One destined to come out on top

In this circus act
I often lose balance
Renting paychecks
I never truly owned

Financial
And mental meet
In a depression
While battling depression

The two converge
The hole goes deeper
Than the eye can see
In the in-between

Within my family tree
Something dark lies in the bark
Dementia runs down
Both sides of my branch

Of all I could forget
I wish to forget the fear
That I too may one day
Forget what it was I feared

The future is scary
The past has left a scar
In between this r and y
Lies the why of my cry

Obstacles
Of my past
And future
Colliding

Parts of me
From the darkest hole
Coming together
As a new whole

Convergence
Is what builds
Mountains
From the Earth

Though these pieces
Of my world
Are crushing me
I hope the summit

Will be worth it

WHAT IT LOOKS LIKE

In March of 2019, I was
Laughing and engaging within a crowd
At a momentous time of my life

If I asked what the scene looked like
You might mention my joy
Or my high energy

Would you notice the monster lurking?
The ventriloquist pulling the strings
Lifting two fingers to feign a smile

Would you notice how the director
Covered a corpse in curtains
To produce an actor

You'd be witnessing a losing battle
An ill-equipped soldier
In an unexpected war

Couldn't name the enemy in the first bout
Until I could … but refused
That would've made it too real

Really, this couldn't be what I thought
Thought it would go away if I pray
Pray that it wouldn't stay

But it did
Set a table
Comfortable

Built a foundation of bended knee
A door of joined palms
Roof of bowed head

This scene
It too
Is what depression looks like

THE PERFORMANCE

Showtime in
Three …
Two …
I …

Have made a performance of living
As a poet, I guess that's the performer in me
Ready to flip a dusty switch
To light up this dead living room

I confide in saying I'm fine
Giving myself time to find what's missing
Wrote a playbill of my life
Called it a resume

Made trinkets
Of my insecurities
Yet still broke since
That don't sell tickets

So, I study a script like scripture

Be "busy," even if not
Have a cover story
In case I'm asked
"How are you?"

Respond with a decoy
Delay the answers
Portray them behind a mic
To bleed out the poison

I've showcased my problems
So much that
They've taken permission
Decided to stay

My anxiety comes on cue
It's never late
For interviews or tests
It's here right now, in fact

I like to think I'm an actor
And how great I feel at the end of filming
Depends on how alive this skeleton appeared to be
Or how big of a smile the sadness can put on

I covered my clown wig
With a church hat on Sundays
But you would never know that
That's how perfect the performance is

So perfect, I never left the stage
The curtains don't fall till the heart stops beating
The mic is attached to my vocal cords
I am the sound system

But not the director
An extra in my own production
The set is mine but I don't feel in control
Empty seats with a sold-out soul

I can uplift your spirits
Yet disregard mine
Your delight
My demise

They intertwine to twist a new reality
Where depression feigns defeat
Pain resembles pleasure
And zombie becomes zealous

That's the thing about theatrics

When the character is so good
You can't see the carcass carrying it
A caricature created
A life behind lies

People tell me
They'd prefer the truth
Of how I feel
Well me too

Who do we think is the first person I lied to?

Denial be the destructive defense
But it's healthy
To make salads of the tomatoes
And a feast of the fright

Might stay in scene all life
Isn't that like a performer?
To give their everything till the very end
Fade to black with no applause promised

When the curtains close
The dialogue dies
And the choreo don't flow
What will the critics say?

This performance …
Was it worth it?

NEVER TOO FAR

My depression says to me ...

"I'M BAAACK!

How you been bro!?
I saw you locked your front door,
so I had to sneak around the back.

I came to check in on you.
That's what best friends do!
Always be there.

I'd say long time no see,
but to be honest I never left.
Didn't want you to miss me.

What's new with you?

I see you still be prayin'.
You wear the evidence of doin' it,
but where's the evidence of it working?

I mean I'm still here right!?
A friend …
treated as foe.

A blessing in disguise that's been denied time and time again.

I should be gone by now
since you don't want me here but,
I'm loyal.

I watched your back,
and removed the knife that you placed there
and passed off as an attack from me.

I'm by your side.

I catch you when loneliness knocks you down.
I pray for you to stay with me,
and you pray me away?

Why do that?
Am I not enough for you?
Am I not everything God is not!?

Claiming He's always there,
but you don't always feel Him.
When I'm there, you ALWAYS feel me!

How's that for consistent?
Stop being resistant
to the connection we have.

You should be thanking me for how strong your faith is.
Instead of praising me away,
praise that I won't leave you astray.

I kept you company when you were bed ridden.
From sunrise to sunset, I didn't leave you.
Yet you blame me for breaking your joy?

How do I damage something that wasn't fixed when I arrived?

You question my intent?
Like I don't have your best interest at heart?
From start to finish I'm there.

Even when you're living on a high.
I was just letting you have your moment.
When you're on top of the world, remember who's waiting at home.

I am not what you're running from,
but what you're running to.
Can't you see me at the finish line, waiting with open arms?

This is a match
too great to be made in heaven.
On a scale of 1 to 10, this is eleven.

This friendship was not diagnosed.
This is organic.
A chemistry that defies the laws of matter.

You're the one with the body, but I'm more real than you are!

More real than the smiles!
More real than the motivational messages!
More real than the dreams you have!

You chase unrealistic goals,
in hopes of leaving behind
the realest thing in your life right now.

Now that's surreal!

You've slept so much to get rid of me,
you can't remember what it's like to be awake.
I know this because I've seen you do it.

Seen you undo alarms.
Wanting hibernation
to yield reincarnation.

A new life.
One without me.
But the longer you lie won't leave me behind.

I've got time.
You're my number one priority.
Tried to leave me back in 2019.

Like a coffin protecting its corpse,
I'm never too far.
That's where best friends are.

Always there.

THE BRIDGE

We are told to never burn

our bridges. What is to keep

them from burying us. On the deck,

where the storm is felt worst. In the center of

my hurricane. Drowning between the oceans of my

eyes. I channel everything within to withstand the quicksand. A sinking captain. Seeking to abandon ship. I peer off the edge in wonder, how if I dissolve in the water below, it'll make a solution. This is a scientific fact … gears back on track. I remember bike rides where I didn't mind if handlebars went a little too far right. Or if a well-positioned rock became the cornerstone to my tombstone. Reaching the destination faster has been more appealing than the journey. My story is on the brink of my firm foundation. I am trusting it will not break. Thankful no more will be on me than I can bear. Though, ungrateful for how enduring these bearings are.

I'm Fine

"I'm fine"

Two words
We use
To wrap our present day
With a bow on top

But what is a gift if not unraveled?

When the facade is lifted
What lies inside
That we keep hidden
To not burden others

Keep this hurt in covers
Can't get burned
If the flame is
Smothered

So … I'm fine

My depression says otherwise
It tries to define me
It defies that I have it
Believes it has me

So finely tuned that
My smile looks real
The finality of this reality is
Solitary confinement amidst a crowd

Joy so overdue I'm indebted with fines
Trying to find peace with two broken fingers
We linger
In this two worded limbo

Until … we finally realize
Even the finest of china
Is made from moldable clay
Diamonds from dirt, thus

Thick skin won't leave me refined
I'll speak as an open book
Won't trade this soft cover for one hard
I'll bare this wear and tear like my Author intended

Feed the flame the oxygen I denied it
Burn finer in it
Stronger because of it
Golden when I'm out of it

It's not yet time but
I will be fine
With saying
"I'm …

… not ok."

THE TUNNEL

When I entered the tunnel
I knew something was wrong
All my life I had at least
Some vision for tomorrow

Suddenly … I saw nothing

Hope for the future
Joy in the morning
Dreams in the distance
Swallowed up by the

Dark

I would give anything
To exit where I entered
But we can't go back
What do we do at a dead end?

If life is a journey
Not a destination
And the path is gone
Before any location

Is it over?

I only packed but
So much for this trip
The baggage is heavy
I'm running on empty

Been wandering
In the shadows
For a while now
Autopilot

This machine is overheating

I'm letting the gears go
Until they are broke
Can't find the off switch
When it is pitch black

Just as my heart is failing
And the walls are closing in
Either my eyes deceive me
Or I finally see …

… light

NO SMOKESCREEN

A Smokescreen is
Designed to hide the truth
Like my mind

When it told me to say
That everything was fine
Until others believed it

Until I believed it

My mind was
A smokescreen
Kept me from seeing how

Depression

Is finding the joy
And meaning in all life
Except my own

Shedding a tear in spring
Not knowing if it's the allergies
Or the sadness

Crying while walking in public
Not meaning to let the pain get out
It is not being able to cry

When I'm ready to let the pressure go

It is the monster
Standing in the corner
Of every room

Growing as I am shrinking
My body deteriorates
A living decomposition

It is time having all control
24/7 Groundhog Day
Yet time still passing by

Deadlines staying the same
While death thoughts get to evolve
And tell me in a different tongue

All the ways I failed

It is sadistic

Killed my productivity
Made me watch
Had me bury the body

Turns my head
To everyone's fingers typing
While mine hover the keyboard

Unable to bring thought to paper
As it whispers
My workload into my ear

It is a breaking point
Getting pushed to the edge
Of the imminent space in my mind

Being at the edge and finding a solution

...

Telling myself
I'll never do it
My reflection tells me to believe that

Where does the smoke end and mirrors begin?

Depression
I don't remember how
Or when you captured me but

April 20th 2019

I told a friend
All that you did to me
And my healing started

I found power out of pain
Peace within the prison
Vision of my ruptured picture

I am a puzzle
The more I'm broken apart
The faster I become at putting the pieces back together

April 22nd 2019

I wrote this poem
On paper I couldn't keep dry
Said a prayer that I once again believed in

The monster
That grew for over 2 months
In the corner of the room

Suddenly began to shrink

It remains there today
Yet it no longer has
Dominion over me

Depression ... I am free

PRESS ON

COMMUNICATE

"Always remember,
you are loved
no matter
what you do.

No shame.
Whatever's happened
I swear worse things
have been done.

There's grace.
For the brokenness,
heartache
and all the pain.

No race.
Breathe.
Take the time you need
as we communicate.

First let me preface,
this world is filled with evil people.
They prey on your prayers.
Drink from your tears.

But that's not on you.

They lie and they lie.
Tell you not to try
to speak about it.
Because they know,

they lose as wounds close.

Though what happened is tragic,
you are still valid.
We're not to blame when
the world takes aim at

our insecurities.

It takes so much heart
to call out depression
and anxiety.
Now we make the choice to

get the help we need.

I know it isn't easy
removing skeletons.
But once the closet's empty
the healing has begun.

If I'm honest, we feel
like we have failed.
How can we improve?
We want you to know

you're not alone.

We're all hurting too.
If it seems we're not there,
trust there's someone
you can turn to.

It will be hard.
This is a start.
Their power
over you

is through."

SOIL

Rock bottom
I am on the floor
Face in the dirt
I am sure I am done

I planted a garden
Looking for a harvest
Drenched it in tears
My fears soaked it up

Nowhere left to turn
I crash and I burn
The ground is filled with doubt
My future can't be found

Maybe now I will learn
Not to have all these

High hopes
Broken goals
Sowing seeds
Reaping weeds

These dreams
Are not Yours they're mine
I wasted the time
On a decline

I landed in pride
Instead of good soil
I cannot grow
If it's not by the Host

What goes up
Must come down
Every bird
Comes to the ground

When I rise
Let it be from You
When I come back
Pray I land it's in good soil

As the earth turns
And the world burns
I know this is true:
It's in You I will grow

You said
Don't fall by the wayside
You said
There's no root in the rockslide

You said
Thorns choke till it all dies
It matters where I'm planted
I must watch where I'm landing

You mean
Seek understanding
You mean
Stand firm in the waves and

You mean
Be in the world, not of it
I must take root
I will be fruitful

METRONOME

When the conductor
Made a constructor
I built a bow from my arm
Strings from the other

For 8 years I was a violinist
Heart pulse in rhythm
Blood pumped on beat
Thoughts born on tempo

Fast forward to college

Head bows in books
Strings lie in silence
Fear fills the void
Dust finds a home

But I still hear the metronome
Tells me to

Keep …
Calm …
Slow …
Down

Amidst runners
It keeps me walking
Amidst future healers
It keeps me healing

Tells me to breathe …
In …
Breathe …
Out

I forget sometimes

Breathing oxygen
Is more important
Than answering oxygen
On the chemistry test I failed …

… or the organic test I failed …

… or the biochem test I failed

This rhythm repeats
I move it FASTER
    But four 8th notes
        Are still 2 beats

Just more notes in a measure
    Just more L's a semester
        Leaving me Lost in a Lyric
            Lagging on Loose Land

Forgetting the first
    Shall be Last
        Thinking the Last
          Shall be Less

Listen I Lie so much
    About my future plans
        Just so people stop asking
            What I'm doing with my life

Sometimes the lies are so good
    Even I believe them
        I forget I'm actually a failure
          A fraud

But fear not
    Anxiety is
        QUICK
            To remind me

I had a panic attack
        Before a meeting I had to lead
           I actually set a timer
               For how long I had to cry

That's what I did in college
        Signed my life away to time
                Maybe that's why the time signature
                        Comes first in music

To remind you
        That your pain
                Isn't yours
                        To schedule

Did you know you can feel claustrophobic in your head?
        Your skull is so busy
                Trying to keep it all together
                        Your brain can't breathe

Adrenaline rushing
        So fast
                You can't feel
                        The open wounds anymore

Wow, it's wild how one fast BEAT
                        Can ruin everything
        I was never good
                At playing 16th notes

                They moved so fast
I always lost control
                I feel
        Like I'm always losing control

I just want it to STOP …

And when it does
I always find myself in bed
Or on a couch
Crying myself to sleep

Funny

When composers can't think of a note
To fill a space with
They tend to think
A rest will solve their problem

Like how I keep thinking
That a rest will fill
The gap that anxiety
Has left in my joy

By the time I realize this …

… the metronome has started again

And I slow …
down …
keep …
calm

Breathe …
in …
breathe …

TRADE

How can I take
all of these ashes
and give them to You
for eternity?

You've seen my worst,
yet claimed it's Yours?
How can I trade
all of these ashes

in for Your beauty?
In for Your mercy?
In for Your power?
In for Your healing?

In for Your blessings?
In for Your grace?
In for the destiny
You said You planned for me?

Ugly ashes.
Beautiful beauty.
Filthy ashes.
Wonderful beauty.

I give You ashes.
You make them beauty.
All my ashes.
Are Your beauty.

So here I take
all of these ashes
and give them to You
for eternity.

You've seen my worst
and claimed it's Yours.
Thank You for
beauty for ashes.

NOTE TO SELF

This is a note to self

Written from your bed
When you had
Another one of those nights

Let this serve
As a reminder
That you are not alone

The length to which you matter
Extends past any deadline
You have missed

You have two hands for a reason

To interlock one with the other
Let the sensation of your touch
Verify your existence

When cold eyes looked around you
Saw through you
Stared at you in dismissal

Know that mine noticed your hands shaking
Your legs shaking
Your heart shaking beneath fragile ribs

When you sink in your chair
And no one pulls you back to surface
I'll breathe for you

I don't need your participation
In the room's conversation
To notice your presence

Your silence speaks volumes to me

I am closer than your shadow
Even in darkness
I am behind you

Ready to catch you when
Temporary pitfalls
Feel like eternal tombs

Look closely

These graves are not yours
I laid death thoughts to rest
For I have seen you at your best

Seen you build a home in Grand Canyon on Monday
Yet plant your garden on Everest by Tuesday
Too often for you to become dormant

You are not doormat
You are not invisible
You are not divisible

You are me
I am you
And I am here for you

With no contracts
No conflicts
No conditions

Signed,

BLIND

My dear child
I know that you
Can't see 2 steps
In front of you

That's the kind of faith
I want for you
So trust and know
I'll show you the way

You feel like life's a mess
But realize that
Puzzles come in pieces
Before the picture is seen

Your greatest masterpiece
Is yet to be redeemed
So trust and know
I'll show you the way

I'll never leave you
I'm by your side
This is your breakthrough
Close your eyes

What I say to you
I will do
I'll be your guide
I'll never hide

Don't need to see
To see that I'm real
20/20 can't prove
All that I can do

Don't need to see
To see that I'm real
2020 can't prove
All that I can do

When lines become blurry
Trust in My story
I've never failed
I never will

Just have blind faith
Don't look at
What's going on
Around you

Just have blind faith
All that glitters
In gold is not
Always true

Your vision can fail you
Mine is good as new
Won't you follow Me?
I'll give you what you need

Just give Me your blind faith

INCREASE

Strength
It is not easy
Carrying a body
Through the journey
Increase

Story
Ink from veins
Pages from pain
Still being written
Increase

Value
Never dies
If they hide yours
Find it, bind it, let it
Increase

Volume
Voice is not Vain
Decibel over decimal
Let no one fraction you
Increase

Belief
Believe
For miracles
To be the normal
Increase

Doubt
Lets you down
Return the favor
And let your faith
Increase

FALL

I go out on a limb
I take a leap of faith
Trusted myself
That's my mistake

I break under pressure
A second too late
With no clear sight I
Took charge of my fate

Face in the ground
A hand reaches down
Lifts me from shame
Grace runs abound

Cracked and broken yet
Value won't decrease
Despite what they say
I choose to believe

To fall is not to fail
It's one letter away
One better way
To stand up again

To fall is not to fail
It's one letter away
One better way
To catch second wind

OASIS

I was on an island
Feeling blue
Thought I was doing good
Though far from home

Was dead inside
Had nowhere to go
That's when You found me
I'm not alone

I was casted
Out into the sea
I lost my way
Stuck in unbelief

Depression came
No way to break free
I couldn't breathe
Lungs filled with grief

Thought I was drowning
From all the shame
But You were drawing
Freed me from pain

Without You I'm nothing
Life would be vain
I was so lost
That's when You said

I'm not raising you
For nothing
Don't you see that
I still care

And now

I'm not sinking
I'm not drowning
I am drinking
From Your fountain

No longer thirsting
You provided
Turned my barren land
To Your Promised Land

Turned my island
To oasis

STAIRS

Elevator?

Stairs?

Society constricts

variety to 1 choice.

Always the elevator.

Never the stairs.

However,

I have forever wanted stairs.

I just want to go upward.

Tired of there being no upward movement.

Living on first floor with no elevator to go higher.

I wanted my own bumpy slide since I was a child.

Thought my mother was wild

demanding no one defile the sanctity the sanctity of her palace.

Now I know the reason it was treason for my friends to visit.

Our kingdom was not like their

castles of multiple levels reached by elevators

I went to college to design a stair blueprint.

Want my parents to get a view from the stairs of my education, before they climb the stairs to heaven.

More than a glimpse from elevation

The sensation of my rise is appearing, can't you feel it?

The noise you hear is me constructing, can't you hear it?

My ascent in life is manifesting, can't you see it?

Blink, and you'll miss this trailer born boy

sitting at the top of the stairs.

Ready for a bumpy slide of his own.

STORMS

I remember safety
I remember joy
Had hope to spare
Strength beyond compare

Then the winds began to blow
Windows I built broke
Trees at my feet
Felt all alone

The sky had a flash
The air had a boom
Took down the guard
Right to my heart

Felt like category seven
Felt like forever
Couldn't see it coming
Came with no warning

Clouds overhead
Lightning striking ground
I lost my way
My path nowhere found

I lost all control …
But that's when You gain control
Turned it around
Reminded me I'm Yours

I'll never forget
I'm loved by the One
Who tells the sun
When to shine

I know You to be
Dependable
I know You to be
All powerful

I remember when
The storms were raging
How you still
Kept me

You are
Keeping me
Always
Keep me

RAIN

In the storm
Don't know which way to turn

Whether left or right
One thing I've learned

Is that all things
Work together

My faith will not change
It's not the weather

I won't be scared
In the flash flood warning

There is no harvest
If it's never raining

All I must do
Is trust and believe

None of Your forecasts
Come back empty

I'll count my wins
In the present

I'll be happy
In the current

As my sins are
Washed away

Till my joy is
Overflowing

I pray my blessings be
Precipitation

It may be stormy
But I am ready

To take joy in the rain
With all the pain

Despite all the shame
There's joy in the rain

CRESCENDO

Quiet
Silence
Is broken
A whisper
Disruption
Brings forth
Construction
Brick by brick
From the ruins
It is building up
A vocal that has
Regained a verse
This stolen sound
Has found its echo
Out of a live burial
Piercing from below
Beyond great measure
Withstanding an erasure
Meant to leave it on mute
Music models a movement
Tone escapes premade tomb
Rumbles from the graveyards
No longer hanging by a thread
Now bellowing through gallows
Reversing a death sentence made
By judges that disregarded its plea
Now free, this testimony soars high
Remembering where its sound began
From lungs that forgot how to breathe
Erupts a chorus that forgets how to end
An audio so stereo it surrounds the noise
Forever to be heard no matter how blurred
Thus teaching the room this important lesson
Ignoring existence doesn't destroy permanence

FOLLOW

You are
Never afraid
To follow me
In the darkest abyss
When I failed
Everyone bailed
You said I'd live
To tell the tale

You are
Never ashamed
To attach
Yourself to me
A sinking ship
You are the captain
You won't abandon
Like in the tale

I was down
Felt alone
No one close
Lost all hope
Out of night
Dawn still breaks
As the light
Chases hate

You follow me

Bottom of the
Barrel
Am not
Beneficial
Have too many issues
With my white flag in hand
As I am walking dead
And even unfollowed

You follow me

No matter
Where I go
You'll be there
To follow
Through the graves
And gallows
I'll be
Safe

PRESS ON

If the average person
Lives 73 years
That amounts to
Over 600,000 hours

Your darkest hour
Is not even
A percent
Of your life

The odds are
In your favor
For things to
Get better

When everything
Tells you the
Opposite
Look at the facts

There's more than
1,000
Ways to die
Every day

Each day that
You draw breath
You have more than
1,000 victories

Every force
That has tried
To take you out
Failed

Your track record
States its case
You have it in you
To finish the race

Should you reach
An impasse
Bury the dead end
Birth a new path

You set the destination
Your traffic can't change it
Your vehicle can't change it
Your detours can't change it

They may affect
Your ETA
But the effect
Stays the same

You will arrive

And when you do
Push open the doors
Pull open the doors
If they won't open

Break down the doors

Move every mountain
Destroy every box
Remove every curse
Breach every wall

And if you fall

Allow yourself to feel
Adapt to the new situation
Activate your ascent and
Always remember

Though this pit
This hole in the ground
This depression
Is deep … press on

I greatly appreciate you taking the time to read my first ever collection!

I believe it was a calling for me to share the messages of this book, and I hope it was a worthwhile experience for you.

Your thoughts, voice and words are valuable to me!

I would be ever so grateful to have a review from you on the Amazon page for this collection, as well as on Facebook.

This, and/or sharing notice of this book would mean everything!

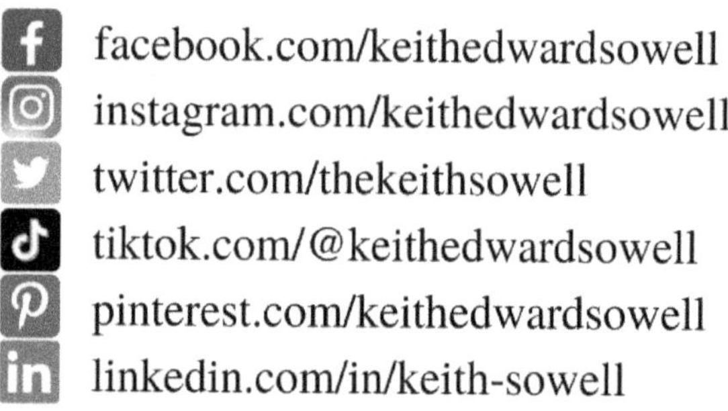

-Keith Edward Sowell

Keith Edward Sowell is a rising poet and spoken word artist from Fayetteville, NC. As a 2020 first-generation alum of Duke University, he has served as publicist and president of the campus poetry collective (Spoken Verb), and captain of the 2019 Duke slam team. He has worked through his alma mater as a College Adviser helping high school students pursue their post graduate goals. Since his undergraduate years and experience on CBS Survivor 38, he has grappled with depression and anxiety. It is from this ongoing battle that he realized: when fallen *Deep, Press On.*

Connect and stay updated with Keith through his website: kesowell.com